11+ English

Year 5-7

Testpack A

(GL Assessment Style)

Practice Paper 1

Please read the following before you start the Practice Paper:

1. Do not begin the Practice Paper until you are told to do so.

2. The Practice Paper contains 49 questions and you have 50 minutes to complete it.

3. Read the questions carefully so that you know what to do.

4. Try and answer as many questions as you can. Do not spend too much time on one question. If you cannot answer a question go on to the next one. If a question is omitted, ensure you have marked it clearly on your question paper, so it is easy to find it when you want to return to it after completing the rest of the paper.

5. If you are doing the Practice Paper as a standard test, circle your answer. If you want to change an answer, put a single line through the wrong answer and circle the correct answer.

    If you are doing the Practice Paper as a multiple-choice test, draw a clear line through your chosen box. If you want to change an answer, rub it out and mark the correct box clearly. **Do not write on or mark the answer sheet in any way other than that which has been specified.**

6. If you finish before your time ends, go back and check your answers.

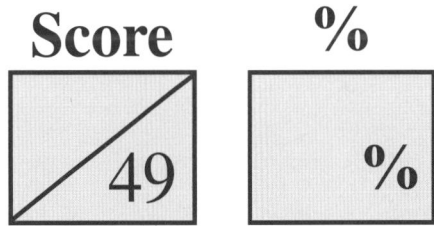

English: Practice Paper 1

SECTION 1: COMPREHENSION

The Call of the Wild

Read this passage carefully and then answer the questions that follow.

The passage you are about to read tells you how life was for a character called Buck at the beginning of the story…and what happened to him at the end.

Buck did not read the newspapers, or he would have known that from Puget Sound in the North to San Diego in the South, trouble was brewing owing to the Klondike strike. In the Arctic darkness, gold had been found, and steamship and transportation companies were looking to profit.

Thousands of men were rushing into the Northland and these men wanted dogs; heavy dogs, with strong muscles with which to toil, and furry coats to protect them from the frost. 5

Buck lived at a big house in the sun-kissed Santa Clara Valley. Judge Miller's place, it was called.

His father, Elmo, a huge St. Bernard, had been the Judge's inseparable companion, and Buck bid fair to follow in the way of his father. 10

He was not so large,—he weighed only one hundred and forty pounds,—for his mother, Shep, had been a Scotch shepherd dog. Nevertheless, one hundred and forty pounds, to which was added the dignity that comes of good living and universal respect, enabled him to carry himself in right royal fashion.

Judge Miller's place stood back from the road, half hidden among the trees. A wide cool 15
veranda ran around its four sides. The house was approached by gravelled driveways which wound about through wide-spreading lawns and under the interlacing boughs of tall poplars.

At the rear were great stables, run by a dozen grooms and boys. There were rows of vine-clad servants' cottages, an endless and orderly array of outhouses, long grape arbours, green pastures, orchards, and berry patches.   20

Then there was the pumping plant for the artesian well, and the big cement tank where Judge Miller's boys took their morning plunge and kept cool in the hot afternoon.

And over all this Buck ruled. Here he was born, and here he had lived the four years of his life.   25

It was true, there were other dogs, but they did not count. They came and went, like the terriers, crowded into kennels. Others remained hidden, like Toots, the Japanese pug, or Ysabel, the Mexican hairless,—strange creatures that rarely put nose out of doors or set foot to ground.

But Buck was neither house-dog nor kennel-dog. The whole realm was his.   30

He plunged into the swimming tank or went hunting with the Judge's sons; he escorted Mollie and Alice, the Judge's daughters, on long twilight or early morning rambles; on wintry nights he lay at the Judge's feet before the roaring library fire; he carried the Judge's grandsons on his back, or rolled them in the grass, and guarded their footsteps through wild adventures down to the fountain in the stable yard, and even beyond, where the paddocks   35 were, and the berry patches. Among the terriers he stalked imperiously, and Toots and Ysabel he utterly ignored, for he was king,—king over all creeping, crawling, flying things of Judge Miller's place, humans included.

Yet Buck was no pampered house-dog. Hunting and similar outdoor delights had kept down the fat and hardened his muscles; and the love of water had been a tonic and a health   40 preserver.

And this was the manner of dog Buck was in 1897, when the newspapers were telling of the Klondike strike.

But Buck did not read the newspapers, and also did not know that Manuel, one of the gardener's helpers, loved to play Chinese lottery and that his gambling had left him short of   45 money.

That was how Buck found himself kidnapped, sold and on his way to the frozen North, where he had many adventures and was often cruelly treated, but eventually found a loving master, John Thornton, to work for.

Buck adored Thornton, but was away hunting a bull moose when the Yeehats (a native tribe)   50 *killed his master...*

The Yeehats were dancing about the wreckage when they heard a fearful roaring and saw rushing upon them an animal the like of which they had never seen before. It was Buck, a live hurricane of fury, hurling himself upon them in a frenzy to destroy…

…Then a panic seized the Yeehats, and they fled in terror to the woods.

They scattered far and wide over the country, and it was not till a week later that the last of the survivors gathered together in a lower valley and counted their losses.

As for Buck, wearying of the pursuit, he returned to the desolated camp. Thornton's desperate struggle was fresh-written on the earth, and Buck scented every detail of it down to the edge of a deep pool, from which no trace led away.

All day Buck brooded by the pool or roamed restlessly about the camp.

Thornton's death left him with a hollow ache inside him that no food could fill. But he was proud of having taken his revenge. From now on he would no longer be afraid of men except when they bore in their hands their arrows, spears, and clubs.

With the coming of the night, Buck became alive to a stirring of the new life in the forest. He stood up, listening and scenting.

From far away drifted a faint, sharp yelp, followed by a chorus of similar sharp yelps that, as the moments passed, grew closer and louder.

Buck walked to the centre of the open space and listened. It was the call of the wild, sounding more compellingly than ever before. He stood, motionless as a statue, waiting the coming of the wolves...

Buck surprised the wolves by attacking but eventually the rest of the pack got him cornered…

…Then Buck recognized the wild brother with whom he had run for a night and a day. He was whining softly, and, as Buck whined, they touched noses.

An old wolf, gaunt and battle-scarred, then came forward. Buck sniffed noses with him, whereupon the old wolf sat down, pointed nose at the moon, and broke into the long wolf howl. Then the others sat down and howled. And so did Buck.

The leaders lifted the yelp of the pack and sprang away into the woods. The wolves swung in behind, yelping in chorus. And Buck ran with them, side by side with the wild brother, yelping as he ran.

An adapted extract from *The Call of the Wild* by Jack London (1876-1916).

English: Practice Paper 1

Answer these questions about the text. Refer back to the text if you need to.

Choose the best answer and draw a line through the rectangle on the answer sheet.

1) Why did Buck not read the newspapers?
    A He didn't have any.
    B He found reading difficult.
    C He was not allowed to.
    D He was a dog.
    E He didn't have time.

2) What was the big news Buck knew nothing about?
    A Gold had been found in the Arctic.
    B Dogs were growing more popular.
    C New rules were being passed.
    D Buck was not wanted any more.
    E Trouble of every kind was brewing.

3) Where was Buck born?
    A In Puget Sound.
    B In San Diego.
    C In Santa Clara Valley.
    D In Scotland.
    E In the Arctic.

4) What kind of dog was Buck's father?
    A A sheep-dog
    B A St Bernard
    C A husky
    D A Japanese pug
    E A Mexican hairless

5) Which of these statements is accurate?
    A The Judge had sons, daughters and granddaughters.
    B The Judge only had sons.
    C The Judge had sons, daughters and grandsons.
    D The Judge only had daughters.
    E The Judge had no sons and two daughters.

MOVE ON TO THE NEXT PAGE

© 2016 Stephen Curran

English: Practice Paper 1

6) Why should Buck have been worried?
   A Dogs with strong muscles and furry coats were urgently wanted.
   B The Judge thought Buck was not the sort of dog he liked after all.
   C The grandsons were afraid of him.
   D He was getting thin.
   E The library fire was bad for him.

7) How did the Judge's sons keep cool in the hot afternoons?
   A They stayed in the shade of the tall poplars.
   B They swam in the cement tank.
   C They played on the cool veranda.
   D They headed for the stables.
   E They picked grapes.

8) Where were the terriers kept?
   A In the servants' cottages
   B In the house
   C Outdoors
   D In kennels
   E Roaming the grounds

9) In what year does the story of four-year-old Buck begin?
   A 1893
   B 1897
   C 1900
   D 1901
   E 1903

10) Who kidnapped Buck and sold him?
    A Elmo
    B Ysabel
    C Mollie
    D Alice
    E Manuel

11) Who was John Thornton?
    A The man who bought Buck after he was kidnapped.
    B The owner of a steamship company.
    C Someone who treated Buck cruelly.
    D A friend of the Yeehats.
    E Buck's loving master whom he adored.

MOVE ON TO THE NEXT PAGE

12) What were the Yeehats doing when Buck attacked?
   A They were out hunting.
   B They were trying to escape from wolves.
   C They were dancing about the wreckage of Thornton's camp.
   D They were celebrating a wedding.
   E They were doing a war-dance.

13) How long was it before the surviving Yeehats got together?
   A Two days
   B A month
   C Half a year
   D A week
   E Three weeks

14) What was Buck proud of?
   A Having had Thornton as a master
   B Having taken his revenge
   C Finding his way back to the camp
   D Being alone
   E Being able to hunt

15) What was 'the call of the wild'?
   A The loneliness.
   B The stirring of the new life in the forest.
   C The coming of night.
   D The yelping of the wolves.
   E The moonlight.

16) How was Buck able to recognise one of the wolves?
   A The wolf was old.
   B The wolf was gaunt and battle-scarred.
   C The wolf pointed his nose at the moon.
   D The wolf howled.
   E It was the 'wild brother' that he had run with for a night and a day.

17) What sign of acceptance did the wolves give Buck?
   A They sat down to rest.
   B They howled.
   C They licked each other.
   D They sprang away into the woods.
   E They pointed their noses at the moon.

MOVE ON TO THE NEXT PAGE

18) What was Buck's place when he ran yelping with the pack?
   A Next to the old wolf.
   B They were trying to escape from wolves.
   C With the leaders.
   D With those at the back.
   E Side by side with the wild brother he had met before.

19) Which of the following gives the meaning of the word 'strike' (line 2) in this context?
   A Refusal to work
   B Punch with a fist
   C Discovery of gold
   D Hit with a club
   E Trains not running

20) What is meant by 'looking to profit' (line 4)?
   A Hoping to make money out of getting more business
   B Hoping to find gold
   C Looking for furry dogs
   D Settling in the North
   E Taking people on their travels

21) What does 'stalked imperiously' (line 36) mean?
   A Crept in with
   B Walked alongside
   C Strode like an Emperor
   D Avoided contact
   E Romped

22) Which of the following is closest in meaning to 'gaunt' (line 76)?
   A huge
   B lean
   C tall
   D mangy
   E grey

23) In the phrase, 'over all this Buck ruled', which of the words is a verb?
   A over
   B all
   C this
   D Buck
   E ruled

MOVE ON TO THE NEXT PAGE

24) What kind of words are these?

Klondike;   Arctic;   Santa Clara;   Judge Miller;   Thornton

   A Verbs
   B Adjectives
   C Common nouns
   D Adverbs
   E Proper nouns

25) How is the quotation, 'a live hurricane of fury' (line 54), best described?
   A A description
   B A phrase
   C A simile
   D A metaphor
   E An analogy

MOVE ON TO THE NEXT PAGE

SECTION 2: SPELLING

In the following passage there are some **spelling** mistakes. In each question there is either **one** mistake or **no** mistakes at all.

Find the group of words which has the mistake in it and mark that letter on the answer sheet.

If there is not a mistake on that line then you should mark N.

School Rules

26) Rules were created to help the school run smoothely and safely. Some children think that they
    A   B   C   D   N

27) were only invented to make life dificult! Here is a list of some rules that we discovered:
    A   B   C   D   N

28) 1. Umberellas can only be brought to school if there is a possibility that the weather will be bad.
    A   B   C   D   N

29) 2. Children are reminded that they are prohibited from running in the coridors at any time.
    A   B   C   D   N

30) 3. All packed lunches will be stored in a cool cupboard at the begining of the day.
    A   B   C   D   N

31) 4. Good behavior is important and everybody is expected to show respect to others.
    A   B   C   D   N

32) 5. Those who repeatedly break the rules could receive a detention and have to remain late.
    A   B   C   D   N

33) Sticking to these rules will help you to have a happy and sucessful time at school.
    A   B   C   D   N

MOVE ON TO THE NEXT PAGE

SECTION 3: PUNCTUATION

In the following passage there are some mistakes in the use of **capital letters** and **punctuation**. In each question there is either one mistake or no mistakes at all.

Fnd the group of words which has the mistake in it and mark that letter on the answer sheet.

If there is not a mistake on that line then you should mark N.

A Wet Lunchtime

34) It was a cold rainy day | and the children sat | around gazing | out of the classroom window.
    A | B | C | D | N

35) "Its' been raining | for hours," moaned Stephanie. | "I wanted to play | outside this lunchtime."
    A | B | C | D | N

36) They had spent the morning, | working on their history project work | and, after that, | they took
    A | B | C | D | N

37) a test on mixed fraction's. | Now all they wanted to do | was to eat their lunch | and run around
    A | B | C | D | N

38) letting off some steam. | Roger and Millie were | trying to play chess, | in the book corner.
    A | B | C | D | N

39) Nathan was so bored | that he decided to continue | working on his project. | What a creep!
    A | B | C | D | N

40) "What do you think | you're doing?" asked Tim. | "Have'nt you done | enough work already?"
    A | B | C | D | N

41) "I've just thought" | said Ann. "We're supposed | to be having games | outside this afternoon."
    A | B | C | D | N

MOVE ON TO THE NEXT PAGE

SECTION 4: CLOZE

Select the best word or phrase to complete the passage so that it is written in correct English and makes sense.

Choose the most appropriate word or phrase from the five choices and mark its letter on the answer sheet.

The Netball Team

42) You have the opportunity [too A] [of B] [with C] [to D] [by E] playing for the school netball team this year.

43) [You'll A] [There B] [You C] [You're D] [They'll E] expected to attend practice after school on Fridays

44) and matches on Tuesdays [whenever A] [wherever B] [because C] [otherwise D] [whereas E] you will be

45) dropped [into A] [onto B] [for C] [under D] [from E] a few weeks. You may only miss a session if you

46) have a good reason and have [bought A] [bringed B] [brung C] [bring D] [brought E] a note from home.

47) You must go to the changing rooms when the bell has [rings A] [ringed B] [rung C] [rang D] [wrung E].

48) Clean kit must be [weared A] [worn B] [wearing C] [warn D] [wear E]. It should be washed at home.

49) Please be careful as last year some of the kit [shrunk A] [shrinked B] [shrank C] [shrink D] [shrunked E] and

we had to spend a lot of money buying new kit for the entire team.

END OF PAPER

11+ English

Year 5-7

Testpack A

(GL Assessment Style)

Practice Paper 2

Please read the following before you start the Practice Paper:

1. Do not begin the Practice Paper until you are told to do so.

2. The Practice Paper contains 49 questions and you have 50 minutes to complete it.

3. Read the questions carefully so that you know what to do.

4. Try and answer as many questions as you can. Do not spend too much time on one question. If you cannot answer a question go on to the next one. If a question is omitted, ensure you have marked it clearly on your question paper, so it is easy to find it when you want to return to it after completing the rest of the paper.

5. If you are doing the Practice Paper as a standard test, circle your answers clearly. If you want to change an answer, put a single line through the wrong answer and circle the correct answer.

    If you are doing the Practice Paper as a multiple-choice test, draw a clear line through your chosen box. If you want to change an answer, rub it out and mark the correct box clearly. **Do not write on or mark the answer sheet in any way other than that which has been specified.**

6. If you finish before your time ends, go back and check your answers.

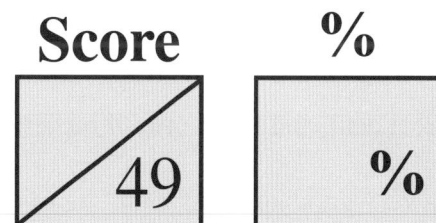

© 2016 Stephen Curran

SECTION 1: COMPREHENSION

Changes in Fortune

Read this passage carefully and then answer the questions that follow.

This story begins in New York, where a young boy has just had a visit from an English lawyer, Mr Havisham, and has found out that he, Cedric Errol, only seven years old, is now a lord, and later on will be an earl!

Cedric's good opinion of the advantages of being an earl increased greatly during the next week. It seemed almost impossible for him to realize that there was scarcely anything he might wish to do which he could not do easily; in fact, I think it may be said that he did not fully realize it at all.

But at least he understood, after a few conversations with Mr Havisham, that he could gratify all his nearest wishes, and he proceeded to gratify them with a simplicity and delight which caused Mr Havisham much diversion.

In the week before they sailed for England he did many curious things.

The lawyer long after remembered the morning they went down-town together to pay a visit to Dick (a young boot-black), and then they so amazed the ancient apple-woman by stopping before her stall and telling her she was to have a tent, and a stove, and a shawl, and a sum of money which seemed to her quite wonderful.

"For I have to go to England and be a lord," explained Cedric, sweet-temperedly. "And I shouldn't like to have your bones on my mind every time it rained. My own bones never hurt, so I think I don't know how painful a person's bones can be, but I've sympathized with you a great deal, and I hope you'll be better."

"She's a very good apple-woman," he said to Mr Havisham, as they walked away, leaving the proprietress of the stall almost gasping for breath, and not at all believing in her great fortune.

"Once, when I fell down and cut my knee, she gave me an apple for nothing. I've always remembered her for it. You know you always remember people who are kind to you."

It had never occurred to his honest, simple little mind that there were people who could forget kindnesses.

The interview with Dick was quite exciting. Dick had just been having a great deal of trouble with Jake, who owned their business, and was in low spirits when they saw him.

His amazement when Cedric calmly announced that they had come to give him what would set all his troubles right, almost struck him dumb.

Lord Fauntleroy's manner of announcing the object of his visit was very simple and unceremonious. The statement that his old friend had become a lord, and was in danger of being an earl if he lived long enough, caused Dick to so open his eyes and mouth, and start, that his cap fell off.

"Everybody thinks it not true at first," said Cedric. "Mr Hobbs thought I'd had a sunstroke. I didn't think I was going to like it myself, but I like it better now I'm used to it. The one who is the earl now, he's my grandpapa; and he wants me to do anything I like. He's very kind; and he sent me a lot of money by Mr Havisham, and I've brought some to you to buy Jake out."

And the end of the matter was that Dick actually bought Jake out, and found himself the possessor of the business and some new brushes and a most astonishing sign and outfit.

He could not believe in his good luck any more easily than the old apple-woman could believe in hers; he walked about like a boot-black in a dream; he stared at his young benefactor and felt as if he might wake up at any moment. He scarcely seemed to realize anything until Cedric put out his hand to shake hands with him before going away.

"Well, good-bye," he said; and though he tried to speak steadily, there was a little tremble in his voice and he winked his big brown eyes. "And I hope trade will be good. I'm sorry I'm going away to leave you, but perhaps I shall come back again when I'm an earl. And I wish you'd write to me, because we were always good friends. And if you write to me, here's where you must send your letter." And he gave him a slip of paper. "And my name isn't Cedric Errol any more; it's Lord Fauntleroy and — and good-bye, Dick."

Dick winked his eyes also, and yet they looked rather moist about the lashes. He was not an educated boot-black, and he would have found it difficult to tell what he felt just then if he had tried; he only winked his eyes and swallowed a lump in his throat.

"I wish ye wasn't goin' away," he said in a husky voice. Then he winked his eyes again. Then he looked at Mr Havisham, and touched his cap.

And when they turned away he stood and looked after them in a dazed kind of way, and there was still a mist in his eyes, and a lump in his throat, as he watched the gallant little figure marching gaily along by the side of its tall, rigid escort.

Until the day of his departure, his lordship spent as much time as possible with Mr Hobbs in the store. Gloom had settled upon Mr Hobbs; he was much depressed in spirits. When his young friend brought the parting gift of a gold watch and chain, Mr Hobbs laid the case on his stout knee, and blew his nose violently several times.

"There's something written on it," said Cedric, "inside the case. I told the man myself what to say.

'From his oldest friend, Lord Fauntleroy, to Mr Hobbs.

When this you see, remember me.'

I don't want you to forget me."
Mr Hobbs blew his nose very loudly again.

"I shan't forget you," he said, "nor don't you go and forget me when you get among the British aristocracy."

"I shouldn't forget you, whoever I was among," answered his lordship. "I've spent my happiest hours with you; at least, some of my happiest hours. I hope you'll come to see me sometime. You — you wouldn't mind my grandpapa's being an earl, would you, I mean you wouldn't stay away just because he was one, if he invited you to come?"

"I'd come to see you," replied Mr Hobbs, graciously.

An adapted extract from *Little Lord Fauntleroy* by Frances Hodgson Burnett (1849-1924) who also wrote *The Secret Garden*.

Answer these questions about the text. Refer back to the text if you need to.

Choose the best answer and draw a line through the rectangle on the answer sheet.

1) *Little Lord Fauntleroy* and *The Secret Garden* were written by which author?
   A Charles Dickens
   B Robert Louis Stevenson
   C E Nesbit
   D Frances Hodgson Burnett
   E Louisa May Alcott

2) The events in the passage take place in which city?
   A New Orleans
   B New York
   C Dublin
   D London
   E Paris

3) Who was Mr Havisham?
   A The boy's father
   B An English lawyer
   C A store-owner
   D The present earl
   E An officer

4) What was Cedric Errol's new name?
   A Dick
   B Hobbs
   C Lord Fauntleroy
   D Havisham
   E Jake

5) What did the seven-year-old lord have trouble in realising?
   A That he could easily do anything he might wish to do
   B That Mr Havisham had travelled to see him
   C That his friends were sad to see him go
   D That Dick's cap fell off
   E That Mr Hobbs would come to see him

MOVE ON TO THE NEXT PAGE

6) How long did Cedric have for saying goodbye?
   A Less than a week
   B Three days
   C Nine days
   D Two weeks
   E A week

7) How were they going to travel to England?
   A By aeroplane
   B By ship
   C By helicopter
   D By canoe
   E On horseback

8) Who was the first friend to benefit from Cedric's good fortune?
   A Dick
   B Mr Haversham
   C Mr Hobbs
   D Jake
   E The apple-woman

9) What was Jake and Dick's business?
   A They were store owners.
   B They were stallholders.
   C They were boot-blacks.
   D They ran errands.
   E They were entertainers.

10) What did Mr Hobbs think must have happened to Cedric?
    A Someone was telling him lies.
    B He had had a bang on the head.
    C There had been a misunderstanding.
    D He was suffering from sunstroke.
    E He had made it all up.

11) Which of Cedric's relations was the earl now?
    A His father
    B His grandfather
    C His uncle
    D His cousin
    E His great-uncle

MOVE ON TO THE NEXT PAGE

12) How did Cedric say goodbye to Dick?
   A He winked at him.
   B He hugged him.
   C He slapped him on the back.
   D He shook hands.
   E He waved.

13) Why did Dick 'touch his cap' (line 53) to Mr Havisham?
   A It was his way of showing respect to a gentleman.
   B He was showing that his cap was now back on his head.
   C He wanted Mr Havisham to have the cap.
   D He wanted Mr Havisham to give the cap to Cedric.
   E He wanted to show he was not stupid.

14) With whom did the young lord spend as much time as possible?
   A Mr Havisham
   B Cedric
   C The apple-woman
   D Mr Hobbs
   E Jake

15) What present did the boy give Mr Hobbs?
   A An apple
   B A gold watch and chain
   C A stove
   D A sign
   E Some brushes

16) What kind of friend did Cedric think he was to Mr Hobbs?
   A His dearest.
   B His greatest.
   C His youngest.
   D His best.
   E His oldest.

17) Why did Mr Hobbs blow his nose?
   A He did not want to be seen crying.
   B He was not paying attention.
   C He had a cold.
   D It was something he had a habit of doing.
   E He wanted to stop a sneeze.

MOVE ON TO THE NEXT PAGE

18) Why might Mr Hobbs want to 'stay away' (line 72) from England?
    A Because he thought his young friend would not want to know him.
    B Because he no longer wished to be friends.
    C Because Cedric's grandfather was an earl.
    D Because he had to stay in New York.
    E Because he couldn't afford the journey.

19) Which is closest in meaning to the word 'diversion' (line 7)?
    A fun
    B amusement
    C happiness
    D bewilderment
    E harm

20) What does 'sweet-temperedly' (line 13) mean?
    A deceitfully
    B proudly
    C boastfully
    D honestly
    E good-naturedly

21) What is meant by 'proprietress' (line 18)?
    A seller
    B owner
    C employer
    D employee
    E maker

22) Which of these words might best be used instead of 'unceremonious' (line 29)?
    A unhesitating
    B humble
    C straightforward
    D speedy
    E informal

MOVE ON TO THE NEXT PAGE

23) How is the quotation, 'like a boot-black in a dream' (line 40) best described?
   A A metaphor
   B A simile
   C A description
   D A phrase
   E A sentence

24) In the phrase, 'It had never occurred to his honest, simple little mind' (line 22), which of the words is a noun?
   A honest
   B occurred
   C little
   D mind
   E simple

25) What type of words are the following?

   wonderful; better; kind; difficult; happiest

   A Verbs
   B Adjectives
   C Adverbs
   D Prepositions
   E Proper nouns

MOVE ON TO THE NEXT PAGE

SECTION 2: SPELLING

In the following passage there are some **spelling** mistakes. In each question there is either **one** mistake or **no** mistakes at all.

Find the group of words which has the mistake in it and mark that letter on the answer sheet.

If there is not a mistake on that line then you should mark N.

The School Trip

26) During the summer term, year six pupils take a trip to the seeside for an environmental studies
   A   B   C   D   N

27) week. It is quite a long journey in the coach and sometimes people suffer from travell sickness.
   A   B   C   D   N

28) Don't think about staying in a hotel, as this is an outdoor camping trip. You have to assemble
   A   B   C   D   N

29) your own tents! There is no television, and radios, computer games and personal sterios are
   A   B   C   D   N

30) not alowed. The meals are prepared on camp stoves by the teachers and the children assist with
   A   B   C   D   N

31) the washing-up afterwards. It's not all fun and games. The trip is surposed to be educational
        A   B   C   D   N

32) and there are worksheets to be completed every day. You do get to work on the beech looking
      A   B   C   D   N

33) for seashells, crabs and intresting pebbles. It's a great way to improve your general knowledge.
       A   B   C   D   N

MOVE ON TO THE NEXT PAGE

SECTION 3: PUNCTUATION

In the following passage there are some mistakes in the use of **capital letters** and **punctuation**. In each question there is either **one** mistake or **no** mistakes at all.

Find the group of words which has the mistake in it and mark that letter on the answer sheet.

If there is not a mistake on that line then you should mark N.

How Time Flies

34) "Isn't it time we went home" said Brian, looking through his pockets to find his watch.
   A — B — C — D — N

35) "We've still got plenty of time," replied Damien. "Its nowhere near five o'clock yet."
   A — B — C — D — N

36) The boys had spent the whole of the afternoon building a secret den in the woods behind
   A — B — C — D — N

37) the old school. Damien had promised that he'd be home by five and would'nt be late.
   A — B — C — D — N

38) Suddenly, there was a loud 'crack' and the sides of the small wooden den began to
   A — B — C — D — N

39) shake violently. The boy's looked at each other in horror. There was panic in their eyes.
   A — B — C — D — N

40) "It's going to fall down. Get out!" Shouted Brian, and they scrambled through the doorway.
   A — B — C — D — N

41) "Boo! shouted Damien's sister, Louise. "Mum's going to kill you. We've been looking for
   A — B — C — D — N

you everywhere. It's almost half past seven! Haven't you got a watch?"

MOVE ON TO THE NEXT PAGE

SECTION 4: CLOZE

Select the best word or phrase to complete the passage so that it is written in correct English and makes sense.

Choose the most appropriate word or phrase from the five choices and mark its letter on the answer sheet.

Sweets!

42) If you ever want to know | where (A) | wears (B) | wheres (C) | where's (D) | wheres (E) | the sweet shop is, you only

43) have to ask my brother, Jason. Nobody is | best (A) | good (B) | better (C) | bestest (D) | goodest (E) | at eating sweets

44) than him. Not | often (A) | likely (B) | ever (C) | quite (D) | only (E) | does he know where all the shops are, but also

45) where any type of sweet is | under (A) | among (B) | behind (C) | between (D) | over (E) | all the others on the shelves.

46) It | would not (A) | should not (B) | could not (C) | did not (D) | does not (E) | do his teeth any good at all.

47) I don't have | much (A) | many (B) | more (C) | fewer (D) | enough (E) | fillings, but Jason has lot and lots. He's

48) been told by the dentist to stop eating sweets | however (A) | cause (B) | otherwise (C) | perhaps (D) | instead (E)

49) all of his teeth might start | to fall out (A) | fall out (B) | falling away (C) | falls out (D) | falls away (E) |!

END OF PAPER

11+ English

Year 5-7

Testpack A

(GL Assessment Style)

Practice Paper 3

Please read the following before you start the Practice Paper:

1. Do not begin the Practice Paper until you are told to do so.

2. The Practice Paper contains 49 questions and you have 50 minutes to complete it.

3. Read the questions carefully so that you know what to do.

4. Try and answer as many questions as you can. Do not spend too much time on one question. If you cannot answer a question go on to the next one. If a question is omitted, ensure you have marked it clearly on your question paper, so it is easy to find it when you want to return to it after completing the rest of the paper.

5. If you are doing the Practice Paper as a standard test, circle your answers clearly. If you want to change an answer, put a single line through the wrong answer and circle the correct answer.

    If you are doing the Practice Paper as a multiple-choice test, draw a clear line through your chosen box. If you want to change an answer, rub it out and mark the correct box clearly. **Do not write on or mark the answer sheet in any way other than that which has been specified.**

6. If you finish before your time ends, go back and check your answers.

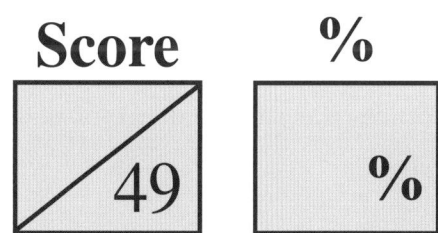

SECTION 1: COMPREHENSION

An Author's Childhood

Read this passage carefully and then answer the questions that follow.

Have you ever stopped to think that all authors of children's books were once children themselves? The stories, adventures and characters in any book you read may give you at least a glimpse of the author's own childhood experiences.

Perhaps you have heard of an author called E Nesbit? Three of her books best known today are: *Five Children and It*, *The Phoenix and the Carpet* and *The Railway Children*. The first dates back to 1902; the second started as instalments in a magazine (1903) and then came out as a book in 1904. In modern times, both these books have been serialised on TV. *The Railway Children* also first appeared in a magazine (1904) and then as a book (1906). In more modern times it has twice been made into a full-length film.

E Nesbit was born in England in 1858 and always wrote under that name even after she became Mrs Bland in 1880. Some readers thought her books were by a man. Actually, E stood for Edith, a popular name for girls in Victorian times.

E Nesbit first wrote poems and stories for adults and her stories for children came later, in the early years of the twentieth century, known as 'Edwardian times'. By 1885, she had three children of her own, but her stories seem to be built very much on memories of the happiest times in her own childhood.

How do we know? Well, although E Nesbit died in 1924, a book based on her reminiscences was published in 1966 and again in 1987, under the title of *Long Ago When I was Young*.

As a child, Edith (who was more often called Daisy!) apparently prayed she would never forget her thoughts, feelings and sufferings, because she felt that her fears, hopes and dreams must be those of every child.

In fact she had a very unusual childhood. During much of the time she had no settled home. Her father had died when she was only three years old. Later, when Edith was between the ages of seven and twelve, her mother had to spend time in France with a much older sister who was not in good health. Edith's two brothers, only a little older than herself, were away at school. Her happiest times were spent with them, when they were able to be together because it was summer and holiday time.

At seven, Edith went to a Brighton school and remembered clearly how mean a certain child was to her. She had reluctantly lent this girl her much-loved miniature tea-service in exchange for a battered doll. When she grew tired of the doll and wanted her pretty cups and saucers back the child spitefully returned them to her in pieces! Edith remembered being too afraid to tell, and that child picked on her many more times.

She was saved from that school by catching measles and when she was better, the family, including her two brothers whom she loved, had a very happy midsummer holiday in a cottage in Buckinghamshire. Edith adored being in the countryside.

Next came another year of difficulty in a new school, this time in Lincolnshire. She describes Miss Fairfield, the owner of the school, as an angel. But 'Miss Daisy' was always being pulled up short by another adult in charge there. Her hair was the sort that never looked tidy and her hands were never clean enough. The punishments were things like doing without a meal, or having breakfast in a cold schoolroom. Sometimes Miss Fairfield would rescue her, giving her bread and jam in secret.

She also remembers long summer days when she was forced to stay indoors and struggle with long division, something she simply could not understand, apparently. Then one evening she heard a carriage arrive and crept across the landing to peep through the banisters at the visitor. It was her mother! Edith would not let go of her and so her mother took her away.

With her brothers gone back to their schools, Edith was taken to France. She writes that Paris was hot and dusty and that the Exhibition left her unimpressed, although she saw the Emperor and Empress and their son, a boy about the same age as herself.

A lot of what she saw as she travelled with her mother and sister frightened her, chiefly because things were not explained to children in those days, and children were not used to talking to grown-ups about how they felt. Her night terrors lasted a long time.

And yet, if you are familiar with the stories she wrote, you will not find such things happening to her characters. It is the happy, family-based times that appear in her books, and the happiest of all was when she and her mother and brothers were together and went to live on a run-down farm near St Malo in Brittany.

But she had more trying times to live through before then.

Once, her mother told her she must have lessons, but instead of being sent to school she was sent to stay with a family where the mother and a little girl of her own age spoke only French. The two girls became friends, and Edith says she learned French in three months.

60

The travelling and some other trying times in schools - in England, France and especially in Germany - all added to her memories. She was always too sensitive to settle away from the family life she longed for.

But the time near St Malo! She describes it as if it were paradise! She and her brothers were pirates and explorers there. They ran free and had great adventures, enjoying the countryside, the freedom and each other's company.

65

Finally she tells of a happy family home in Kent, where she had a room of her own and could dream all she liked.

E Nesbit always enjoyed writing and had a poem published when she was only fifteen.

70

When she finally began her children's stories it was not only because she enjoyed writing them but also because, like her character called 'Mother' in *The Railway Children*, she needed to make money.

Authors generally do lots of reading and Edith was no exception. She also had a vivid imagination and a love of fantasy and magic as is clear from the stories she created.

75

———————————————————————

Answer these questions about the text. Refer back to the text if you need to.

Choose the best answer and draw a line through the rectangle on the answer sheet.

1) Why does the passage remind you that all authors were children once?
   A It means they understand all children.
   B They know how long each book should be.
   C They must therefore like children.
   D Their books may tell you about their own childhood.
   E They have the right to publish books.

2) When was *Five Children and It* first published?
   A 1902
   B 1903
   C 1904
   D 1905
   E 1906

3) What has happened to *The Railway Children* in more modern times?
   A It has not been read much.
   B It has been read by more children than ever before.
   C It has twice been made into a full-length film.
   D It has been found too hard to understand.
   E It has disappeared from libraries.

4) In which year was E Nesbit born?
   A 1858
   B 1880
   C 1885
   D 1924
   E 1966

5) The initial E in E Nesbit was short for which popular girl's name?
   A Elspeth
   B Edith
   C Eleanor
   D Elizabeth
   E Ethel

MOVE ON TO THE NEXT PAGE

6) E Nesbit's children's books were written in which times?
    A Modern
    B Victorian
    C Ancient
    D Prehistoric
    E Edwardian

7) What different name does the author say she was called as a child?
    A Ellie
    B Daisy
    C Victoria
    D Angel
    E Patricia

8) Where did she go to school when she was seven?
    A Brighton
    B Lincolnshire
    C France
    D Germany
    E Buckinghamshire

9) What was little Edith lent in exchange for her tea-service?
    A A new doll
    B A paint-box
    C A pretty doll
    D A battered doll
    E A book

10) What made it easy for the other girl to pick on Edith again?
    A They were often alone together.
    B Edith was a new pupil.
    C Edith was younger.
    D The other girl was always allowed to do as she liked.
    E Edith was too afraid to tell.

11) How did Edith get away from that school?
    A It was the end of term.
    B They did not want her there.
    C She caught measles.
    D There was no one to pay for her.
    E Her place was needed for someone else.

MOVE ON TO THE NEXT PAGE

12) In what kind of house did the family live in Buckinghamshire?
    A A big house
    B A farm
    C A town house
    D A cottage
    E A flat

13) Who owned her next school?
    A Miss Daisy
    B The 'adult in charge'
    C Edith's mother
    D Edith's sister
    E Miss Fairfield

14) Why did Edith get punished?
    A For untidy hair and dirty hands
    B For not being dressed properly
    C For not being able to do her sums
    D For being cheeky
    E For being bad at games

15) What secret food was sometimes given to her?
    A Breakfast in a cold schoolroom
    B Porridge
    C Cake
    D Bread and jam
    E Chocolate

16) How did Edith persuade her mother to take her away?
    A She promised to be good.
    B She said she would like to travel.
    C She said she would like to learn French.
    D She would not let her go.
    E She wanted to see the Emperor.

17) Why did Edith get so frightened at things she saw?
    A Things were not explained to children in those days.
    B It was planned that way.
    C She said she was so young.
    D She was in a foreign country.
    E There were no other children with her.

MOVE ON TO THE NEXT PAGE

18) Where did Edith experience the happiest of times?
   A All over France
   B In a new school
   C On a rundown farm in Brittany
   D In Germany
   E At the last school she went to

19) Which of these words could best take the place of 'not in good health' (line 26)?
   A stupid
   B crazy
   C unwell
   D sorrowful
   E absent-minded

20) Which word is closest in meaning to 'reluctantly' (line 30)?
   A gladly
   B unwillingly
   C graciously
   D proudly
   E slowly

21) Which of these best describes the meaning of 'miniature' (line 30)?
   A minute
   B brand-new
   C sculptured
   D expensive
   E rare

22) What is meant by Edith's 'love of fantasy' (line 75)?
   A She wrote about history.
   B She was not truthful.
   C She lived in a daydream.
   D She described ordinary events.
   E She liked to write about strange things happening.

MOVE ON TO THE NEXT PAGE

23) Which of the words, 'She writes that Paris was hot and dusty' (lines 48-49), is a proper noun?
   A She
   B writes
   C Paris
   D hot
   E dusty

24) What type of words are the following?

   became;   wrote;   wanted;   travelled;   began

   A Verbs
   B Adjectives
   C Adverbs
   D Conjunctions
   E Nouns

25) How is the quotation, 'She and her brothers were pirates and explorers' (lines 65-66) best described?
   A A simile
   B An analogy
   C A description
   D A metaphor
   E A phrase

MOVE ON TO THE NEXT PAGE

SECTION 2: SPELLING

In the following passage there are some **spelling** mistakes. In each question there is either **one** mistake or **no** mistakes at all.

Find the group of words which has the mistake in it and mark that letter on the answer sheet.

If there is not a mistake on that line then you should mark N.

Auditions

26) The St Mark's School anual musical is very popular. All the children can audition for a part,
    A   B   C   D   N

27) althrough they must be good singers and be prepared to do some energetic dancing as well.
    A   B   C   D   N

28) Those wanting to take part must attend a spechal rehearsal organised by Mrs Thomas, the
    A   B   C   D   N

29) music teacher, and Mr Brown, the drama teacher. Each child must sing a verse from a poplar
    A   B   C   D   N

30) song and read some lines from the story. The teachers then have a discussion and deside who
    A   B   C   D   N

31) should be in the musical. I can't sing so I definately won't get a part this year. Fortunately, I
    A   B   C   D   N

32) won't be left out as there are millions of other jobs to do. I could help to piant the set or
    A   B   C   D   N

33) operate the lights. The school is buzing with excitement. This year's musical will be fabulous.
    A   B   C   D   N

MOVE ON TO THE NEXT PAGE

SECTION 3: PUNCTUATION

In the following passage there are some mistakes in the use of **capital letters** and **punctuation**. In each question there is either **one** mistake or **no** mistakes at all.

Find the group of words which has the mistake in it and mark that letter on the answer sheet.

If there is not a mistake on that line then you should mark N.

A Bad Night

34) Tom wasn't the type of boy / who was easily frightened, / but he'd sometimes / get nightmares
   A / B / C / D   N

35) that seemed so, very real. / There was one bad dream / that occurred / over and over again.
   A / B / C / D   N

36) He dreamt that he was / standing at one end of / a long corridor and / could see a tall slim,
   A / B / C / D   N

37) figure in the distance / walking towards him. / It looked like mrs Balderstone, / the head
   A / B / C / D   N

38) teacher. She would / call his name in a / loud rasping cackle. / "Tom!" she'd screech,
   A / B / C / D   N

39) "I want to see you. / I want to talk to you, Tom. / Didn't you hear me. / I want to talk to you."
   A / B / C / D   N

40) Tom wanted to run, / but he could'nt. / His feet were stuck as if / glued to the floor. There was
   A / B / C / D   N

41) no escape, / He could only shut his eyes / as the teacher approached / and said in a low menacing
   A / B / C / D   N

voice, "Why are you in school? It's Saturday today!"

MOVE ON TO THE NEXT PAGE

SECTION 4: CLOZE

Select the best word or phrase to complete the passage so that it is written in correct English and makes sense.

Choose the most appropriate word or phrase from the five choices and mark its letter on the answer sheet.

Party Time!

42) James had been | worker | worked | work | working | works | with his father to empty the garage
                      A   B   C   D   E

43) ready for the party | although | unless | whilst | until | because | his mother didn't want a mess
                            A   B   C   D   E

44) made in the house. They put in the CD player and | sting | strunged | strung | stringed | strings |
                                                         A   B   C   D   E

45) up some lights. James was | excitingly | excitedly | exciting | excited | excitely | awaiting the
                                    A   B   C   D   E

arrival of all his school friends for the 'best party of the year'.

46) " | There'll | Their'll | There | They'll | Their | be here soon," he said. "I wrote four-thirty on the
          A   B   C   D   E

47) invitations." He had | spent | spending | spend | spended | spends | hours making them last week.
                              A   B   C   D   E

48) "They | shant | wouldn't | won't | can't | couldn't | be coming at all," said Dad, looking at
              A   B   C   D   E

49) the invitation. "This | said | says | saying | sayed | siad | Sunday. Today's Saturday!"
                              A   B   C   D   E

END OF PAPER

11+ English

Year 5-7

Testpack A

(GL Assessment Style)

Practice Paper 4

Please read the following before you start the Practice Paper:

1. Do not begin the Practice Paper until you are told to do so.

2. The Practice Paper contains 49 questions and you have 50 minutes to complete it.

3. Read the questions carefully so that you know what to do.

4. Try and answer as many questions as you can. Do not spend too much time on one question. If you cannot answer a question go on to the next one. If a question is omitted, ensure you have marked it clearly on your question paper, so it is easy to find it when you want to return to it after completing the rest of the paper.

5. If you are doing the Practice Paper as a standard test, circle your answers clearly. If you want to change an answer, put a single line through the wrong answer and circle the correct answer.

   If you are doing the Practice Paper as a multiple-choice test, draw a clear line through your chosen box. If you want to change an answer, rub it out and mark the correct box clearly. **Do not write on or mark the answer sheet in any way other than that which has been specified.**

6. If you finish before your time ends, go back and check your answers.

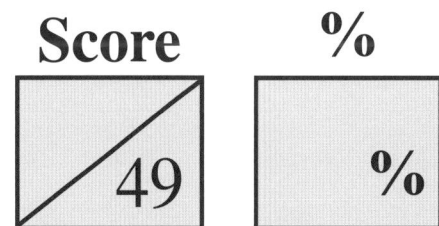

© 2016 Stephen Curran

SECTION 1: COMPREHENSION

The Legend of the Aegean Sea

Read this passage carefully and then answer the questions that follow.

A Greek legend

'This must be the wettest half-term ever,' thought Connor. He had done no exploring. Still, tomorrow he would be seeing his beloved great-grandfather, John, with whom he shared a love of maps.

Connor got out his collection. Between Greece and Albania, he found the Aegean Sea, and wondered how it had got its name. He could try the internet or wait until the next day, because John would be sure to know the story. He would have learned it at school.

Connor was right...

"There's a very famous legend about it," said John, "an exciting adventure, but with a sad ending."
"Please! I'd love to hear it," said Connor.

And John began to tell the ancient Greek tale of *Theseus and the Minotaur*.

Long ago in Athens there lived a king's son called Theseus, who was already a hero having done many brave deeds.

Now Minos, king of Crete, had conquered the Athenians, and he had made a hard and cruel peace. Every year the Athenians had to send seven young men and seven maidens to be sacrificed to a monster called the **Minotaur***, who lived in a place called the* **labyrinth***, a winding path among rocks and caves. The young people chosen must go on board a ship with black sails, and journey to Crete to be torn to pieces!*

Theseus was determined to rid his father's people of this horrible evil. One spring when the herald from King Minos arrived, Theseus went and told his father, Aegeus, that when the black-sailed ship set out next morning he would go too and slay the Minotaur.

"But how?" said Aegeus, knowing his son must be cast to the monster defenceless like the rest. And Theseus said, "Are there no stones in that labyrinth, and have I not fists and teeth?"

Aegeus clung to him weeping bitterly but at last agreed, having made him promise that if he succeeded, he would take down the black sail of the ship and hoist a white one for the voyage home; that way his father, watching from the cliffs, would know his son was safe.

In the market place, the people stood weeping.

"I myself will be one of the seven youths!" cried Theseus. The herald was amazed and asked if he knew what would happen to him.
"I know," said Theseus.

As they went on board he whispered to his companions, "Have hope, for the monster is not immortal."

And so they sailed away to the palace of Minos, the great king, who was rumoured to have been taught by Zeus himself, chief of the Greek gods.

The young Athenians were brought before the king who ordered them to be thrown to the monster one by one. But Theseus begged to be the first, as he had chosen to come of his own accord.

He told the king, "I am the son of your enemy, Aegeus, king of Athens, and I have sworn that I will not go back till I have seen the monster face to face."
"Take the madman away," said Minos, frowning; and Theseus was led away with the rest.

But Ariadne, Minos' daughter, loved him for his courage and his majesty. And by night she went down to the prison, and told him: "Flee down to your ship at once, you and all your friends, for I have bribed the guards before the door. But take me with you! For if I stay my father will kill me."

Theseus was confounded by her beauty, but answered, "I cannot go home in peace till I have seen and slain this Minotaur and put an end to the terrors of my land."

Then Ariadne asked him how he would kill the monster and afterwards find his way out of the labyrinth and, seeing the hero was relying merely on his boldness and strength, she gave him a sword to help him attack. And, to mark the way back, she gave him a ball of thread, known as a clue. And Theseus gladly promised to take the fair princess with him back to Greece.

Then evening came and the guards led him away to the labyrinth...

"Tea's ready," announced Connor's mother.

"Thank you, Mary," said the old man, who loved to eat with his family.

Connor knew he would just have to wait to find out more. John never shortened a tale or gave anything away.

After tea, Connor listened as his great-grandfather continued the story.

Theseus went left and right, up and down among the rocks and caverns, till his head was dizzy (but still held his clue with its thread that he had fastened to a stone as he went in) until at last he met the Minotaur. The strange beast had a man's body, but the head of a bull, and the teeth of a lion for tearing his prey.

The Minotaur roared, lowered his head and rushed right at Theseus, who nimbly stepped aside, and cut him in the knee as he passed. The path was too narrow for the monster to turn and Theseus followed him, stabbing him again and again from behind, till he fled, bellowing wildly; he had never before been wounded. And Theseus followed him at full speed, holding the clue in his left hand.

Both rushed on through one cave after another, then on up Mount Ida to the edge of the snow.

And at last Theseus came up with him, caught him by the horns, and forced his head back, driving the keen sword through his throat. Then he turned and, following his thread, came limping and weary to where Ariadne waited.

"It is done!" he whispered, and they went and set all the prisoners free, then leapt on board and escaped to Naxos where Ariadne became Theseus' wife...

"That's a *happy* ending!" cried Connor.

"Haven't you forgotten about the Aegean Sea?" queried John, ignoring the interruption. Connor nodded.

"Well," continued the storyteller, "Ariadne never came to Athens. Some say Theseus left her sleeping and a god called Dionysus took her up into the sky.

"However it happened, Theseus, grief-stricken, forgot his promise to his father. And so Aegeus, straining his eyes to catch sight of the ship, saw the black sail and believed Theseus to be dead.

"And, in his misery, he fell into the sea, and died; which is why that sea is known as *the Aegean* to this day."

"Thank you for telling me," said Connor. "I love your stories."

Yet part of him wished he had never asked.

Answer these questions about the text. Refer back to the text if you need to.

Choose the best answer and draw a line through the rectangle on the answer sheet.

1) What kind of weather was spoiling Connor's holiday?
    A Snowy
    B Very wet
    C Changeable
    D Cold
    E Windy

2) What had Connor really wanted to do?
    A Read books
    B Meet friends
    C Be with his family
    D Explore
    E Study

3) Why was Connor especially glad John was coming the next day?
    A John was his great-grandfather.
    B He had not seen him for a long time.
    C He wanted to talk about maps.
    D He liked having tea with him.
    E He wanted to find out how the Aegean Sea got its name.

4) How had John come to know his stories?
    A He was very old.
    B He had read a lot.
    C He had learned them at school.
    D He had worked as a storyteller.
    E He liked stories.

5) Why was Connor's great-grandfather reluctant to tell the story?
    A The tale had a sad ending.
    B It was about an exciting adventure.
    C He was not sure he could remember it.
    D It was too long.
    E It was frightening.

MOVE ON TO THE NEXT PAGE

6) For which reason was Theseus already known as a hero?
   A He was an Athenian.
   B He had done many brave deeds.
   C He was a king's son.
   D He was a young man.
   E He was angry that Athens had been conquered.

7) What was the 'horrible evil' (line 19) affecting the people of Athens?
   A They were under attack.
   B Every year they had to face their enemy again.
   C A monster was threatening them.
   D They had to send seven youths and seven maidens to be sacrificed to the Minotaur.
   E They had to send a black-sailed ship to Crete.

8) Which of these is true of the Minotaur?
   A It was impossible to describe.
   B It was a sort of dragon.
   C It had the head of a bull on a man's body.
   D It was totally unlike a man.
   E It was a kind of lion.

9) Who was Minos?
   A The king of Athens.
   B The king of Crete.
   C A Greek god.
   D The herald who arrived each spring.
   E The monster.

10) Who was Theseus' father?
    A Aegeus
    B Zeus
    C Minos
    D Dionysus
    E John

MOVE ON TO THE NEXT PAGE

11) What did Theseus tell his father he wanted to do?
- A Rescue the young Athenians from the ship
- B Do battle with his father's conqueror
- C Kill the Minotaur to stop any more young Athenians being sacrificed
- D Stop the black-sailed ship from sailing
- E Send the ship back to Crete with no-one on board

12) What part of the story indicates the hero was unlikely to succeed?
- A His father reminded him he had to meet the Minotaur 'defenceless'.
- B He would not be wearing any armour.
- C The Minotaur had never been beaten.
- D He did not know if he would be the first to be thrown to the monster.
- E It would be getting dark.

13) Why did Theseus think he still had a chance?
- A He was brave and strong.
- B He could use his fists, teeth and any stones lying around.
- C Someone would be bound to help him.
- D The Minotaur might possibly leave him alone.
- E There might be special rules for him.

14) Theseus made a promise to his father. What was that promise?
- A He must return at once.
- B He must bring back the head of the Minotaur.
- C He must kill the king of Crete as well.
- D He must marry one of the seven maidens.
- E He must hoist a white sail on his returning ship.

15) What unexpected event worked in Theseus' favour?
- A The king of Crete would not let him be thrown to the Minotaur.
- B Theseus never found the Minotaur.
- C Theseus was indeed strong enough to defeat the Minotaur.
- D The Cretan princess, Ariadne, fell in love with him.
- E Ariadne was locked up in the prison with him.

MOVE ON TO THE NEXT PAGE

16) The tale was interrupted before John had finished. What was the reason?
    A John had got tired.
    B Connor was bored.
    C John decided to end the story another day.
    D Connor's mother said tea was ready and Connor knew he must wait.
    E John was going home.

17) In his encounter with the Minotaur, Theseus made an early move that eventually led to the Minotaur's death. Which of the following best describes what Theseus did?
    A He attacked first and killed the monster at once.
    B He stepped aside as the monster rushed right at him.
    C He avoided a headlong attack and wounded the monster's knee.
    D He used a stone to throw at the monster.
    E He tied his thread to a stone as he went in.

18) Which of these best indicates how hard it was to find a way out of the labyrinth?
    A 'a winding path among rocks and caves' (lines 16-17)
    B to mark the way back ... a ball of thread' (line 49)
    C 'Theseus went left and right, up and down among the rocks and caverns, till his head was dizzy' (lines 57-58)
    D 'Through the cave after another' (line 66)
    E 'And at last Theseus came up with him' (line 67)

19) What does 'immortal' (line 32) mean?
    A Able to stay alive for ever
    B Unconquerable
    C Unable to be wounded
    D Able to kill all comers
    E Knowing everything

20) What is meant by 'of his own accord' (lines 36-37)?
    A With permission
    B At his own expense
    C Alone
    D Without being made to
    E As the king's son

MOVE ON TO THE NEXT PAGE

21) Which is closest in meaning to the word 'keen' (line 68)?
    A eager
    B solid
    C sharp
    D short
    E light

22) Which word or phrase is closest in meaning to 'grief-stricken' (line 77)?
    A Miserable
    B Full of sadness
    C Overcome with sorrow
    D Lonely
    E Unable to think

23) Which of the words in the phrase, 'limping and weary to where Ariadne waited' (line 69), is a verb?
    A and
    B weary
    C where
    D Ariadne
    E waited

24) Which of these is an adjective?
    A sailed (line 33)
    B fair (line 50)
    C whispered (line 70)
    D sacrificed (line 16)
    E misery (line 80)

25) What type of words are the following?

    Courage;   majesty;   boldness;   strength;   speed

    A Common nouns
    B Adjectives
    C Abstract nouns
    D Verbs
    E Conjunctions

MOVE ON TO THE NEXT PAGE

SECTION 2: SPELLING

In the following passage there are some **spelling** mistakes. In each question there is either **one** mistake or **no** mistakes at all.

Find the group of words which has the mistake in it and mark that letter on the answer sheet.

If there is not a mistake on that line then you should mark N.

My Saturday Morning

26) I love Saturdays. Even though there is no school I am frequently very busy and must organise
   A — B — C — D — N

27) my time carefully so that I can fit everything in. After breakfast I go to the garage and check
   A — B — C — D — N

28) my bicycle. I have a lot of traveling to do and cycling is the quickest way to get around.
   A — B — C — D — N

29) I take my backpack and head off to the library to exchange my books. I prefer reading fiction.
   A — B — C — D — N

30) My next stop is Grandad's house. He always gives me pocket money to by sweets with!
   A — B — C — D — N

31) To get to the sweet shop, I cut through the alley at the end of the road, avoiding all the obsticles
   A — B — C — D — N

32) as I don't want to get a puncture. Walking home with a flat tire is ever so embarrassing!
   A — B — C — D — N

33) By eleven o'clock I am on my way home. Ocasionally it is necessary to stop at the supermarket
   A — B — C — D — N

to buy some food for Mum. I wouldn't get any lunch otherwise!

MOVE ON TO THE NEXT PAGE

SECTION 3: PUNCTUATION

In the following passage there are some mistakes in the use of **capital letters** and **punctuation**. In each question there is either **one** mistake or **no** mistakes at all.

Find the group of words which has the mistake in it and mark that letter on the answer sheet.

If there is not a mistake on that line then you should mark N.

A Visit from Grandma

34) "Your grandma's coming to stay," announced Mum one morning at breakfast. "She'll be
     A   B   C   D   N

35) arriving on wednesday and staying for a few days. You know what we need to do."
     A   B   C   D   N

36) Grandma was Jenny's father's mother and was extremely fussy. She could'nt resist making
     A   B   C   D   N

37) remarks that upset Mum. If there was one spot of dust then Grandma would find it and point
     A   B   C   D   N

38) it out For the few days before each visit Mum, with Jenny's help, would clean the house
     A   B   C   D   N

39) from top to bottom. Jennys' bedroom had to be cleaned, tidied and fresh sheets put on the
     A   B   C   D   N

40) bed for Grandma. Jenny would have to share her little sister Bethanys room, whilst Grandma was
     A   B   C   D   N

41) in the house. Mum was very grateful. "You are such a treasure" she told her daughter.
     A   B   C   D   N

MOVE ON TO THE NEXT PAGE

SECTION 4: CLOZE

Select the best word or phrase to complete the passage so that it is written in correct English and makes sense.

Choose the most appropriate word or phrase from the five choices and mark its letter on the answer sheet.

The Intruder

42) Mr Johnson was [awake A] [awaked B] [awoked C] [awoken D] [waked E] by a loud noise coming from

43) outside in the garden. He immediately [springed A] [sprang B] [sprunged C] [springs D] [springing E] out of

44) bed and headed downstairs to [look A] [looked B] [see C] [saw D] [seen E] what was going on. He

45) only paused to put on his dressing gown. His wife [lies A] [lays B] [layed C] [lade D] [lay E] in bed still

46) asleep. "There's somebody out there," he [thought A] [thanks B] [thinks C] [thinked D] [thinking E] to

47) himself. "[Whom's A] [Whose B] [Who's C] [Whom D] [What's E] out there?" he shouted as he peered

48) into the garden. He could see something moving around [into A] [over B] [between C] [above D] [across E]

the dustbins. Suddenly a pair of bright, shining eyes stared straight at him. Mr Johnson smiled to

49) himself as the red fox [quickest A] [quickly B] [more quickly C] [most quick D] [quick E] ran away.

END OF PAPER

Multiple-choice Answer Sheets

11+ English Year 5-7 Testpack A Practice Paper 1

Section 1: Comprehension - *The Call of the Wild*

Question	Options
1	A B C D E
2	A B C D E
3	A B C D E
4	A B C D E
5	A B C D E
6	A B C D E
7	A B C D E
8	A B C D E
9	A B C D E
10	A B C D E
11	A B C D E
12	A B C D E
13	A B C D E
14	A B C D E
15	A B C D E
16	A B C D E
17	A B C D E
18	A B C D E
19	A B C D E
20	A B C D E
21	A B C D E
22	A B C D E
23	A B C D E
24	A B C D E
25	A B C D E

Section 2: Spelling - *School Rules*

Question	Options
26	A B C D N
27	A B C D N
28	A B C D N
29	A B C D N
30	A B C D N
31	A B C D N
32	A B C D N
33	A B C D N

Section 3: Punctuation - *A Wet Lunchtime*

Question	Options
34	A B C D N
35	A B C D N
36	A B C D N
37	A B C D N
38	A B C D N
39	A B C D N
40	A B C D N
41	A B C D N

Section 4: Cloze - *The Netball Team*

Question	Options
42	A B C D E
43	A B C D E
44	A B C D E
45	A B C D E
46	A B C D E
47	A B C D E
48	A B C D E
49	A B C D E

Section 1: Comprehension - *Changes in Fortune*

1	2	3	4	5	6	7
A	A	A	A	A	A	A
B	B	B	B	B	B	B
C	C	C	C	C	C	C
D	D	D	D	D	D	D
E	E	E	E	E	E	E

8	9	10	11	12	13	14
A	A	A	A	A	A	A
B	B	B	B	B	B	B
C	C	C	C	C	C	C
D	D	D	D	D	D	D
E	E	E	E	E	E	E

15	16	17	18	19	20	21
A	A	A	A	A	A	A
B	B	B	B	B	B	B
C	C	C	C	C	C	C
D	D	D	D	D	D	D
E	E	E	E	E	E	E

22	23	24	25
A	A	A	A
B	B	B	B
C	C	C	C
D	D	D	D
E	E	E	E

Section 2: Spelling - *The School Trip*

26	27	28	29	30	31	32	33
A	A	A	A	A	A	A	A
B	B	B	B	B	B	B	B
C	C	C	C	C	C	C	C
D	D	D	D	D	D	D	D
N	N	N	N	N	N	N	N

Section 3: Punctuation - *How Time Flies*

34	35	36	37	38	39	40	41
A	A	A	A	A	A	A	A
B	B	B	B	B	B	B	B
C	C	C	C	C	C	C	C
D	D	D	D	D	D	D	D
N	N	N	N	N	N	N	N

Section 4: Cloze - *Sweets!*

42	43	44	45	46	47	48	49
A	A	A	A	A	A	A	A
B	B	B	B	B	B	B	B
C	C	C	C	C	C	C	C
D	D	D	D	D	D	D	D
E	E	E	E	E	E	E	E

11+ English
Year 5-7
Testpack A
(GL Assessment Style)
Practice Papers 1-4

Answers and guidance notes for parents

These practice papers can be completed as standard or multiple-choice tests.

Multiple-choice Tests
Your child should mark their answers on the multiple-choice answer sheets. It is important for them to treat it like the real thing and record an answer in the appropriate box by drawing a clear line through their chosen box with a pencil. Clarity is important as the actual test would be marked by a computer. Mistakes should be carefully rubbed out and not crossed out since this would not be correctly recorded by the computer.

Standard Tests
Ask your child to circle the answers in each section. Mistakes should be crossed through with a single line and the correct answer circled.

Marking and Feedback
The answers are provided in this booklet. Only these answers are allowed. One mark should be given for each correct answer. Do not deduct marks for wrong answers. Do not allow half marks or 'benefit of the doubt', as this might mask a child's need for extra help in the topic and does not replicate the real exam conditions. Always try to be positive and encouraging. Talk through any mistakes with your child and work out together how to arrive at the correct answer.

Timing
Each test should take 50 minutes, however it is more important that a child completes the test accurately and does not rush. Children will speed up naturally with practice.

Score	%	Score	%	Score	%	Score	%	Score	%
1	2%	11	22%	21	43%	31	63%	41	84%
2	4%	12	24%	22	45%	32	65%	42	86%
3	6%	13	27%	23	47%	33	67%	43	88%
4	8%	14	29%	24	49%	34	69%	44	90%
5	10%	15	31%	25	51%	35	71%	45	92%
6	12%	16	33%	26	53%	36	73%	46	94%
7	14%	17	35%	27	55%	37	76%	47	96%
8	16%	18	37%	28	57%	38	78%	48	98%
9	18%	19	39%	29	59%	39	80%	49	100%
10	20%	20	41%	30	61%	40	82%		

© 2016 Stephen Curran

Answers

Practice Paper 1

1) D	14) B	27) B	40) C
2) A	15) D	28) A	41) A
3) C	16) E	29) D	42) B
4) B	17) B	30) D	43) D
5) C	18) E	31) A	44) D
6) A	19) C	32) N	45) C
7) B	20) A	33) C	46) E
8) D	21) C	34) A	47) C
9) B	22) B	35) A	48) B
10) E	23) E	36) B	49) C
11) E	24) E	37) A	
12) C	25) D	38) C	
13) D	26) C	39) N	

Practice Paper 2

1) D	14) D	27) D	40) B
2) B	15) B	28) N	41) A
3) B	16) E	29) D	42) A
4) C	17) A	30) A	43) C
5) A	18) C	31) C	44) E
6) E	19) B	32) D	45) B
7) B	20) E	33) B	46) E
8) A	21) B	34) B	47) B
9) C	22) E	35) C	48) C
10) D	23) B	36) N	49) A
11) B	24) D	37) D	
12) D	25) B	38) N	
13) A	26) C	39) B	

Answers

Practice Paper 3

1) D
2) A
3) C
4) A
5) B
6) E
7) B
8) A
9) D
10) E
11) C
12) D
13) E
14) A
15) D
16) D
17) A
18) C
19) C
20) B
21) A
22) E
23) C
24) A
25) D
26) B
27) A
28) B
29) D
30) D
31) C
32) D
33) B
34) N
35) A
36) D
37) C
38) C
39) D
40) B
41) A
42) D
43) E
44) C
45) B
46) D
47) A
48) C
49) B

Practice Paper 4

1) B
2) D
3) E
4) C
5) A
6) B
7) D
8) C
9) B
10) A
11) C
12) A
13) B
14) E
15) D
16) D
17) C
18) C
19) A
20) D
21) C
22) C
23) E
24) B
25) C
26) C
27) A
28) B
29) C
30) D
31) D
32) C
33) B
34) N
35) A
36) D
37) B
38) A
39) B
40) C
41) C
42) D
43) B
44) C
45) E
46) A
47) C
48) C
49) B

PROGRESS CHARTS

Practice Paper 1

Technique Used

1-25	Comprehension	(25)	_____
26-33	Spelling	(8)	_____
34-41	Punctuation	(8)	_____
42-49	Cloze	(8)	_____

Total Score _____
Percentage _____%

Practice Paper 2

Technique Used

1-25	Comprehension	(25)	_____
26-33	Spelling	(8)	_____
34-41	Punctuation	(8)	_____
42-49	Cloze	(8)	_____

Total Score _____
Percentage _____%

Practice Paper 3

Technique Used

1-25	Comprehension	(25)	_____
26-33	Spelling	(8)	_____
34-41	Punctuation	(8)	_____
42-49	Cloze	(8)	_____

Total Score _____
Percentage _____%

Practice Paper 4

Technique Used

1-25	Comprehension	(25)	_____
26-33	Spelling	(8)	_____
34-41	Punctuation	(8)	_____
42-49	Cloze	(8)	_____

Total Score _____
Percentage _____%

Overall Percentage [____%] For the average add up % and divide by 4

If your child needs to revise any topics or techniques, please refer back to the Essential Workbooks in our English Comprehension series:

Workbook 1
Basic Approaches to Text
Probing the Text
Analysing Prose
Analysing Poetry
Comprehension Questions

Workbook 2
Reading the Text
Comparing Texts

© 2016 Stephen Curran

CERTIFICATE OF

This certifies

_____

has successfully completed

11+ English
Year 5-7
TESTPACK **A** PAPERS **1-4**

Overall percentage score achieved ☐ %

Comment _____

_____

Signed _____
(teacher/parent/guardian)

Date _____